Praise for the work of Norbert Krapf

In half a lifetime of writing history and poetry about the Catholic communities of the Jasper [Indiana] area and their German antecedents, Krapf has shown a sense of place and ethnic identity that radiates out to universal brotherhood. In [*Blue-Eyed Grass: Poems of Germany*], he reminds us of the all-American Walt Whitman, who remained "a part of all that I have met"; and of Wendell Berry, who sings of his beloved Kentucky that he has seen the worst and best of humankind there.

—*The Indianapolis Star*

With its emphasis on the specificities of a place and its people, Krapf's poetry has deep affinities with the local color tradition of American literature. But like Kentucky poet Wendell Berry, Krapf's forte is in recognizing the spiritual interaction between a people and their place. . . . For Krapf, the relationship is that of a son who has been much blessed through the sacredness of place and familial love.

—*Sycamore Review*

"One place comprehended can make us understand other places better," Eudora Welty writes in one of her essays. Welty's statement finds ample support in Norbert Krapf's *Somewhere in Southern Indiana*. Although these poems are deeply rooted in the landscape of southern Indiana and the lives of Krapf's German-Catholic ancestors, their ultimate concerns are what Faulkner called "the old universal truths" of "love and honor and pity and pride and compassion and sacrifice."

—*Arts Indiana*

Dr. LaVern J. Rippley
Editor SGAS Newsletter
St. Olaf College - German Dept.
Northfield, MN   55057-1098

The Country I Come From

Also by Norbert Krapf

Poetry

–Limited Editions–

The Playfair Book of Hours (1976)
Arriving on Paumanok (1979)
Lines Drawn from Dürer (1981)
Heartwood (1983)
Circus Songs (1984)
A Dream of Plum Blossoms (1985)
East of New York City (1986)
March Songs for an English Half-Moon (1988)

–Trade Editions–

Somewhere in Southern Indiana: Poems of Midwestern Origins (1993)
Blue-Eyed Grass: Poems of Germany (1997)
Bittersweet Along the Expressway: Poems of Long Island (2000)

Memoir

The Sunday Before Thanksgiving: Two Prose Memoirs (1998)

Translator/Editor

Beneath the Cherry Sapling: Legends from Franconia (1988)
Shadows on the Sundial: Selected Early Poems of Rainer Maria Rilke
    (1990)

Editor

Finding the Grain: Pioneer Journals, Franconian Folktales, Ancestral
    Poems (1977)
Under Open Sky: Poets on William Cullen Bryant (1986)
Finding the Grain: Pioneer German Journals and Letters from
    Dubois County, Indiana (revised and expanded edition, 1996)

The Country
I
Come From

Poems

Norbert Krapf

Archer Books

Published in 2002 in the United States by
Archer Books
P. O. Box 1254
Santa Maria, CA 93456
www.archer-books.com
info@archer-books.com

Distributed in the United States by
Midpoint Trade Books
New York, NY
www.midpointtrade.com

First Edition

Cover photo: *Cornfield at Sunset, C.R. 600 near Freeman, Owen
County* © 1995, 2002 by Darryl Jones

Author photo: © 2000, 2002 by Andreas Riedel

Cover design: JTC Imagineering

Library of Congress Cataloging-in-Publication Data

Krapf, Norbert, 1943-
The country I come from : poems / Norbert Krapf.
p. cm.
ISBN 1-931122-05-9
1. Indiana--Poetry. I. Title.

PS3561.R27 C68 2002
811'.54--dc21

2002021554

in memory of my mother,
Dorothy Schmitt Krapf
(1913-1997),
source of many poems

Acknowledgments

Some of these poems originally appeared, sometimes with a different title and in different form, in the following publications: *Amelia* ("The Language of the Species"), *American Scholar* ("The Mandolin and the Tenor"), *Arts Indiana* ("Full Circle," "Lines Heard in Northern Indiana Cornfields"), *Blueline* ("Bloodroot," "Places," "Queen Anne's Lace"), *Caffeine Destiny* ("The Morning Glories"); *Cottonwood Review* ("Mississenewa Field Shrine"), *ELF: Eclectic Literary Forum* ("Gathering Hickory Nuts," "Woods Hymn"), *The Heartlands Today* ("The Corn Cave," "Hayloft," "Pastoral Poetics," "When the House Was New"), *Forkroads* ("The Horseradish Man"), *Long Island Quarterly* ("Feeding the Cattle," "Hauling Hay," "Milk Music," "The Potato Barrows"), *Midwest Poetry Review* ("Adam Schmitt's Plums," "The Blackberry Bramble," "The Labor Day Boxes," "The Martin Box"), *Poetry Tonight* ("Dream of a Hanging Curve"), *Texas Quarterly* ("Mississsinewa Cottonwood Leaf," "A Whiff of Fresh Sheets"), *32 Pages* ("The Language of Place," "Odysseus in Indiana," "Return to a Mighty Fortress," "Saturday Night at the Calumet"), and *Western Humanities Review* ("Song for Bob Dylan"). Thanks to the editors of these little magazines for their support.

"Sassafras" and "White Oak" were included in the author's *Heartwood* (Stone House Press, 1983). *One Voice from Many* was written for the occasion of the 100th commencement of St. Joseph's College, Rensselaer, Indiana, and distributed 7 May 1995 as a pamphlet to those who participated in that happy event. "Fire and Ice" won the 1999 Lucille Medwick Memorial Award of the Poetry Society of America judged by Toi Derricotte. Jeanetta Calhoun, James Alexander Thom, and Stewart Rafert deserve thanks for blowing quiet whistles that led to revisions of poems in the first section. Thanks to Bob Dylan for his words and music that have provided inspiration and sustenance over the decades, his repeated rebirths as an artist just as critics and followers proclaimed him dead, and the line in "With God on Our Side" that suggested my Midwestern title.

Once in his life a man ought to concentrate his mind upon the remembered earth, I believe. He ought to give himself up to a particular landscape in his experience, to look at it from as many angles as he can, to wonder about it, to dwell upon it. He ought to imagine that he touches it with his hands at every season and listens to the sounds that are made upon it. He ought to imagine the creatures there and all the faintest motions of the wind. He ought to recollect the glare of noon and all the colors of the dawn and dusk.

N. Scott Momaday, *The Way to Rainy Mountain*

One's native ground is the place where, since before you had words for such knowledge, you have known the smells, the seasons, the birds and beasts, the human voices, the houses, the ways of working, the lay of the land, and the quality of light. It is the landscape you learn before you retreat inside the illusion of your skin. You may love the place if you flourished there, or hate the place if you suffered there. But love it or hate it, you cannot shake free. Even if you move to the antipodes, even if you become intimate with new landscapes, you still bear the impression of that first ground.

Scott Russell Sanders, *Staying Put*

Contents

III. Odysseus in Indiana

The Country I Come From

Prologue: A Whiff of Fresh Sheets

Reading in warm June sun
a Kiowa's poems about
the spirit of a mythic bear
who lives and looms
in memory and imagination

when a breeze from the south
blows up a whiff reminiscent
of fresh white sheets dried
and bleached in the sun
on my mother's clothesline
in southern Indiana
almost fifty years ago

and I am carried back
a thousand miles by this breeze
and that fresh scent still
lodged in my nostrils

though she is gone
to the world of spirit
and the house we built
at the edge of the woods
has passed out of our hands

and I am there again
sent with a basket
to gather the wash
and I bury my face
in the white folds
of those fresh sheets
and inhale as deeply
as one can draw air

and the scent of the sun
into his lungs

and the taste and smell
of sun and fresh air
in the folds of those sheets
fill and lift and transport me

and I return decades older
to the page where the tracks
of the bear cross the page
in June sun and fresh breezes
blow across the German lupine
and columbine in my garden.

I

The Language of Place

Full Circle

To wind up the hills
from Louisville, the Ohio
River bending at your back,
is to enter southern Indiana
once again and see out
of the corner of your eye
the red-tail hawk soar in its
eternal circle over the valley
split right down the middle
by the meandering creek
on the banks of which
the ivory sycamore prevails

is to notice dark-green
cedars appear on either side
of the sloping interstate
like shy friends from childhood
you thought you had forgotten

is to come into the presence
of the delicate rust
of prairie grass rippling
and rolling in the breeze
as a cottontail bounds
up the hill toward the horizon
beyond which some part of you
that has lain dormant knows
every angle and every grade
of every curve and awakens
and tugs and pulls you home.

The Language of Place

You have no name for it
but feel it pull on you
when you enter the hills,
like a forgotten language
a part of you spoke
thousands of years ago.

By studying you cannot
recover what has been lost,
but must let it rise
up from the landscape
and allow it to speak
in that part of the ear
that never unlearned
how to listen to what
is deepest as you give
yourself to the pull
of the place.

The way a creekbed
meanders through a hollow,
a breeze scrapes dry corn
leaves against one another,
a mulberry tree stands
at the bottom of a well
of sunlight on a hill
beside a sagging barn
built on a site where
hunters once camped
as they traveled along
the ridges the glacier left

may give off syllables
that gather into words

that build into sentences
that carry a meaning
you intuit but could
not translate for others

unless you feel the ancient
rhythm and ritual of prayer
suddenly rise up from
the ground and pass
through and beyond you.

The Language of Species

You want to make
a convincing statement
but all you can see
is the outline of a forest.

Wait. Don't speak. Move in.
Stand there as long as it
takes for the dark to lift
from your shoulders and light
to flicker on your forehead.

Look up. Watch a single tree
take shape and rise. Allow
the bark of the trunk time
to declare its texture.
Watch a leaf push forth
as a pattern. Listen to breezes
wash through the boughs.
Follow cuttings as they sprinkle
down through layers of leaves.
Trace the stream back to the source:
hungry fox squirrel or blackbird.

Now say what you see.
Say shagbark hickory.
Say pig hickory or walnut.
Say beech or black gum.
Say white or red oak.

When you can speak
the language of the species
others may listen and believe.

What We Lost in Southern Indiana

In 1800 swollen streams & the Buffalo Trace
ran through forests almost impenetrable.
Here & there, marshes. Birds that love a forest
& those that love water found a home.

The wild turkey was so plentiful we sometimes
shot it from our cabin door. You could kill
a dozen in a day & exchange them for salt
at Vincennes. Squirrels were so thick we shot

them to save our few fields of ripening corn.
The Carolina paraquet, long since disappeared,
we found in large flocks in low land around
Duck & Buffalo Pond. The Piankashaw used

their red, green & yellow feathers as ornaments.
Wild pigeons flocked by in clouds that darkened
the sky. People brought torches to their roosts
& waged war on the blinded birds with clubs & guns.

Hundreds were killed that nobody could use.
Red deer cut paths across divides in the hills,
& to springs & "licks" in the valleys. Once
the deputy clerk of Dubois County shot two

deer from his office window as they ran down
Main Street, Jasper. When we killed a deer
in those days, we took only the skin and the ham.
The women cooked venison & turkey by hanging

it beneath a slab of bear meat dripping grease.
Bears were abundant, & left the imprint of their

powerful claws on the barks of huge trees. Deep
in the woods we would find bear wallows clawed

out of the soft floor of a cave. Wild hogs roamed
the woods in such great numbers they were a threat
to human life. At Halls Creek Bottom, where they fed
on mast & roots, a settler once lost his life to their

viciousness. Wild hogs were so common we waited
until they grew fat & took as many as we wanted.
No one seemed to care. The wolf was a terrible menace.
Wolves under two months brought a dollar; those older,

two. To claim this bounty, a hunter had to produce
the wolf scalp & both ears. Hunters would find
a den, catch the puppies, make them cry,
& shoot the mother as she came running home.

The Buffalo Trace

Before European metal wedged
    into native poplar, before wagons
        rolled up from Kentucky, buffalo

would loll in herds in Indian
    summer sun chomping sweet
        grass on the prairie to the west

until their stomachs expanded
    and tongues longed
        to lick a coarser substance.

They turned in unison from
    the setting sun, splashed across
        the Wabash River and plunged

headfirst into the forest where
    maple leaves flared red and their
        hooves pounded hickory nuts

that rattled to the ground. Twisting
    and turning into the depths
        of the forest like a great storm

that leaves a clearing in its wake,
    they spiraled southeast, churned
        across the White River, drummed up

the hillsides and along the ridges,
    stampeded downhill through the valleys
        until heading into the rising sun they

slowed down, sank to their knees
in the Ohio, floated like shaggy ships
across to Kentucky, and coasted

to Big Bone and Blue Licks in bluegrass
country. There in a sea of brown fur they
scraped pink tongues across white salt

in the springs and heaved against
one another in the winter swamp until
they sank down pressed beneath the hooves

of those that came after them year by year
bones packed in layers like stones in pave-
ment that cannot be lifted from their beds.

What the Miami Call Themselves

When they lived
in what we name
Wisconsin and Michigan,
before they moved
southeast to what we
now know as Indiana,
the Ojibwa called
them *Oumameg*,
"people of the peninsula."

Their closest allies,
the Delaware,
the Lenni-lenape,
called them
We-mi-a-mik,
Wemiamick,
"all friends" or "beavers."

The French, who
married their daughters,
referred to them
as *Oumiamiouek*
or *Oumiamiak*
and *Monami*,
"my friend."

The English, ever
in love with
their own tongue,
called them
Twightees,
"the cry of the crane."

In the *Me-ah-me*
or *Meame* tongue,
meeneea or *meearme*
means "pigeon."

They call themselves
Wa-ya-ta-no-ke
or *Me-a-me-a-ga*,
"nation born from
eddying water."

When they came southeast
to the Indiana Territory
they settled in the town
of *Kekionga*, "blackberry
patch," on the Maumee,

and gravitated toward
the eddying waters
of creeks and rivers we call
Wabash and Wea and Eel
and the swift Mississinewa
which carved caves we know
as their sacred Seven Pillars
before joining forces
and becoming one
with the Wabash,

Wah-bah-shi-ki,
Wah-bah-shay-ke,
Wah-sah-shay-ke,
Wa-ba-ci-ki
or *Waubache*,

"white or pure bright water,"
"water flowing over white stones,"
"white path," or "white like
the inside of a mussel shell."

Miami Words into English

"The last children who spoke the Miami language
into adulthood were born in the 1870s,
assuring the eventual death of the language."
—Stewart Rafert, *The Miami Indians of Indiana:*
A Persistent People 1654–1994 (1996).

From the time of the fur trade:
a dollar, *ngoti mäkwa*, one beaver;
a quarter, *ngotiäsepana*, one raccoon.

From the time when the men
worked in the circus
that wintered near Peru:
an elephant, *wapingwilokia*,
a "white skin";
a monkey, *alalaciwia*,
"always hunting lice";
a lion, *kinozawia*,
"long yellow hair."

Translated from Miami compounds
for Anglo-Saxon things:
carpenter, "makes anything";
coffee, "bean liquor";
mule, "long ears";
beer, "foaming water";
gold coins, "yellow money";
silver coins, "white money."

The title of the autobiography
of William Peconga (1844–1916),
grandson of Meshingomesia,
atotamané, "I tell my life story."

Song of the Mississinewa

Na-ma-tei-sin-wi,
Na-ma-chis-sin-wa,
Mas-pis-sin-e-way,
the Miami called it,
"much fall in the water,"
"falling water," or
"it slopes and slants."

Villages that stood
along the water way
that sings and falls
and rises and bends
were *Washashie,*
Meshingomesia,
Metosanya.

Mis-sis-sin-e-way,
we who came later
from far away
have said and spelled it,
Massassinawa,
Mississinway,
Mississineway.

See its waters flow
and fall and foam
and you will fall
in love with its
shape and rhythms.

Say it and you will
know what it means
to sing a song
hear a music
feel a spirit
that can never
be taken away:

Mississinewa.

Mississinewa Field Shrine

Big puffballs
  of thistle beaming
    purple atop tall stems

    twined with green vines,
  arrow-shaped leaves
& wide-open cups

of morning glory white
  dripping with dew
    below tufts

    of pine needles
  swaying & touching
in the breeze.

The Mississinewa at Night

In the heavy dark where you stand
  under cottonwoods the water rushes
  white ashore onto limestone slabs

  slides back out into the depths
  where it swirls & turns & rejoins
the current & heaves & bucks

its way downstream toward
  the Miami Port that has become
  Peru past a series of caves where

  spirits convene across from which
descendants still camp & if you
sound the river's name with respect

Mis-si-sin-e-wa, Mis-si-sin-e-wa
  you will hear a slow song of liquid
  syllables roll like the waters from

  your tongue & lift the darkness
in which you stand & look as currents
rush by rippling & reflecting the moon.

Mississinewa River Lament

1

At dusk, white Queen Anne's lace
and goldenrod guard the gravel
parking lot. The shallow woods
are silent except for the bump
and buzz of mosquitoes. Between
the trees stand separate monuments
to U. S. soldiers and Indian warriors
and a dozen tombstones glowing
white on a knoll: twelve carved
names of whites who died (but are
not buried) here in 1812. Not one
piece of stone, not a single name,
to honor the Miami women
and children who died here
in their village. Not far away,
below a stand of ancient sycamore,
the river with the sibilant name,
source of secrets, still sings
its syllables of lament.
White shoals, luminous, break
over limestone shelves at dusk.

2

Next morning I return, haunted,
in broad daylight. Queen Anne's
lace, thistle in purple bloom,
morning glory twining
stalks of thistle, blue chicory,
and goldenrod. Mosquitoes
remain the only visitors.

In the woods, many locusts,
spikes climbing their trunks.
Slippery elm, cottonwood.
The liquid Mississinewa looks
even more dazzling in daylight.
I walk down to water's edge,
stand on limestone shelves,
see boulders stretching across
to the other side downstream.
What was it like to leapfrog
from one to another? What
was it like to live in a village
so carefully situated here?

I think of a bitter December
day when old men, women,
and children gather around
a fire to talk and do chores.
In their daydreams, it is summer.
Old men fish in the shoals; women,
singing, gather herbs in the woods;
children play games on the bank.
Corn, squash, and beans grow
in a field beyond the knoll.

Suddenly it is again cruel winter,
the insides of my nostrils freeze,
and I hear the crack of rifles,
the cries of children, the clomp
of hooves on brittle earth.
The smell of smoke hangs
in arctic air, rolls out over
a choppy Mississinewa.

What was it like to return
home from the hunt to find
your village smoldering in ashes,

woman and children slaughtered,
red pools frozen beside them?

Who or what twisted a language
capable of carrying the truth
home to the heart with such beauty,
grace and power as to call this
"The Battle of the Mississinewa"?

Mississinewa Cottonwood Leaf

Along the river
of five syllables
I pick this heart
from a branch
of a tree rooted
in a holy place
& press it
in a notebook.

When I return
one year later
to reopen the pages
& revisit the scene
where Miami & Delaware
gave their lives
to save a village

I admire the saw-like teeth
edging the green heart
& the S-curve, bending
like a river, of its delicate
stem which I lift
& spindle in the air.

When the heart cracks
in the middle & crumbles
into my hand I hear liquid
syllables speak again within
white shoals near those woods

and know I must
compose this song
to carry the spirits
of the past

into the present
so they can flow
toward the future.

Lines Heard in Northern Indiana Cornfields

Rensselaer, August, 1993

Be glad for moisture
hanging above
and beaded below,
for the color gray
in the sky,
for flat land where
corn & soybean touch
& stretch to a copse
of spectral trees
on the horizon.

Watch for the sway
of Queen Anne's lace
in early breeze
and the surprise
of backlit morning glory
twining around weed
and stalk of corn.

Acknowledge the blessing
of chicory blue
& soybean green.

Pause before a single
sunflower that took
a bright stand
a stone's throw
into a splash
of weeds.

Listen to what does
not seem to speak.

Keep an eye open
for what is thought
not to blossom.

Appreciate shades
of color that
do not flash.

Inhale air that
does not aim
to uplift because
all is level
unto the horizon.

Carry the plenitude
of plainness
with a bounce
of joy.

Give thanks
for the wealth
of the ordinary
rolling in from
cloudy gray across
prairie green.

Mayapple

for Rose Marie and John Groppe

Walking down an abandoned road
toward a boarded-up brick house,
once a home for Indian children,
I look up in the Sunday morning
hush and see mayapple green
whirling and rolling toward
the edge of the woods where
shopping center asphalt begins.

I kneel down at the side
of the road to peer beneath
this low canopy of green
and find a creamy flower
with a center as golden
as fresh butter holding what
light seems left in the world.

From a nearby stalk hangs
a tiny green apple that
has already passed through
flowering and come to rest
poised as ripe fruit.

At the base of stalks
coming up out of the ground
in every direction violets
beam their modest blue.

Whorls of green spikes
for which my tongue
cannot shape the praise
of a name slant toward
the pull of light and poke

through slits in the canopy.

A thatch of dead brown leaves
on the ground grows luminous.

I rise back to my feet
quivering with thanks
for the gift my legs
have brought to my eyes.

Fire and Ice

Dead of winter: snow, ice,
winds lashing the plains
of frozen northern Indiana.

The brick fieldhouse
of the Catholic college
that admitted only men roared
like an overheated furnace.

Poles, Irish, and Italians
from the cities around
the Great Lakes, a few
Germans from the hills
to the south along the Ohio,
we stretched our vocal chords
to the snapping point as our
team scratched, slipped,
rallied and finally failed
against Lutheran archrivals.

When we entered the igloo
of our freshman dorm
someone, incensed, found
rays of light escaping
into the hall from beneath
Leland Richard's door.

Leland was a black intellectual
from Cleveland who had dared
to stay home and not support
the holy communal cause.

Maybe he was reading a book,
writing a letter to his family
or just wanted to be alone.

Maybe he was thinking about
what to do with his life.

Someone knocked on the door.
No answer. Someone pounded.
Still no answer. "Stayed
in his room during the game!"
echoed down the hall. Someone
brought a can of lighter
fluid and squirted it under
the door. Someone else struck
and flipped a match. Flame
zigzagged under the door that
bitterly cold night as someone
chanted "Spear chucker!"

I stood there watching,
listening from a distance
while my friend sat alone
trapped between fire and ice.
I could not find whatever
words should have come out.

Leland never once mentioned
that night when we later sat
in the cafeteria discussing
literature and foreign films.
I could never bring myself
to ask how it felt to watch
flame shoot beneath his door,
hear the chant from beyond.

Two springs later after green
flames lit brown grass around
the pond in front of the chapel
with the postcard twin towers,
Leland entered a seminary.
I never heard from him again.
I have just learned he is dead.

One Voice from Many

Written for the 100th Commencement
of St. Joseph's College, Rensselaer, Indiana
7 May 1995

1

To come here from the hills
of the south to these plains
of the north was to bring
with you the voices
of those who came before
even though you did not
know they spoke within you.

For to learn how to read
the world opening before you
like the pages of a book
that you must translate from
more languages than one
is to learn to hear
the nuances of pitch
the beat of accent
and the turn of idiom
of the various voices
others help us to detect
as we grow toward
the single voice
integrated from the many
who came before and shape
the sound of what we say
as we discover the feel
of what we believe
on the way toward finding
who we shall become
and the mission of what

we must do to leave
something to hear, see,
and feel for those who
shall come after us
and become a part
of what we are.

2

When he came north
from the hills to the flat
cornfields where fierce
winter winds howl
as he had never heard
wind howl before, he did
not follow anyone in his
family to a degree or hear
any voice speak from within
his past to make him think
he might find a language
to speak beyond himself.

He came as the son of a father
who wept when he had to stop
school after eight and one half
years but could read and speak
German. He came as the son
of a mother named Schmitt
who finished high school early
after fooling a jealous big sister
by hiding high in the branches
of a maple in front of the farmhouse
to read James Whitcomb Riley,
but could not afford college.

He saw no poetry books
on the shelves of their house
and heard no poets talking

to one another across the ages,
to friends and family in his
hometown, or to himself.

When he came here he followed
others from the hills to the south
with unliterary names like Brosmer,
Gutgsell, Hoffman, Hollinden, Krodell,
Pfeffer and Roos. He came with buddies
named Backer, Betz, Eckerle and Spindler
who also missed the curves of hills.

He looked around and found classmates
from Chicago, Cleveland, and Cincinnati
who told him their families' stories at night
in the dorm: Herbst, Hattemer, Koenig,
Kuemmerle, Muth, Reichert and Schultz.
Putting their names together he did not
hear the smooth music of the poems
he began to read in textbooks,
but a collision of consonants
and the kick of a beat he felt
pound right beneath his ribs.

He looked up to new instructors
named Groppe, Herzing and Rank
who loved the ways of words
and helped him hear how they
whispered together and built
to a crescendo. He studied
under priest-professors Druhman,
Esser, Gerlach, Kramer, Kuhns
and Lang who put his fingertips
on the pulse of the past.

He stacked a semester of German
atop an overload, under a priest
named Hiller who corrected his

pronunciation of words he voiced
as he had overheard them said
at the supper table, in the streets
of Jasper and across the fields
of Dubois County. Reciting
the language of his ancestors
he sometimes heard a murmur
that seemed to rise up from
and through those who had
come and gone before him.

3

He remembers lying in the green
grass of his freshman spring
in front of campus buildings
as fresh breezes blew by
reading the Russian Dostoevski
in the grip of a fever that
has never released its hold.

He remembers standing transfixed
in the hall of a brick building
since burned to the ground
as a shaft of sunlight found
the page he was reading
of a long poem by Walt Whitman
of Long Island which included
no German names in his catalogues
of ordinary Americans and his
litanies of their everyday activities.

He remembers discovering
the passion and power
of the written word
as passport to a world beyond
wooded hills and cornfield plains.

But he did not write the word
except in letters to friends,
a few stories and poems
he hid in a drawer, and journal
entries he kept to himself.

He had not found a voice
which could reach back
to include those who came before
and could not presume to speak
to or for anyone but himself
as he moved on and away.

4

To come back here today
from Walt Whitman's island
extending east of Manhattan
to celebrate your going forth
as you stand where I stood
thirty years ago almost to the day

is to witness a new present
in the act of being born
and to speak in a voice
layered with the memory
of what has gone before

is to say that the past
you shall discover
in the process of going
where you must go
in building the present
that will shape a future

is to see that you
shall become a part
of those who will

come here after us
and discover that
our pitch, our accent,
our very idiom

will be heard within
the communal voice
that shall one day speak
to the many who follow.

II

When the House Was New

Pastoral Poetics

"Beetles rolling balls of dung."
—Walt Whitman

Summer afternoons on the farm
where my mother grew up
I would walk down the rock road
barefoot with a cousin to bring
the cows home from pasture.

To have your feet in shape
meant the bottoms had become
so thick and tough you could
walk on almost anything
without feeling pain.

Even if your feet were in shape,
you had to be careful where
you walked after you turned
into the pasture because
of what you might step into
and what might then squish
up between your toes.

You had to look down
when you were about
to step, even as you
looked over the hill
for a herd of cows.

Once I looked down and saw
a black beetle rolling a ball
it had shaped from a rich
brown platter. I couldn't
believe any creature would
take the time to make

such an attractive shape
out of waste that had passed
through another creature
and have the patience
to roll it across a pasture
where two barefoot boys
were looking for cows.

Years later when I read
a long poem by Walt Whitman
I couldn't believe I had found
a poet who actually looked down
at the ground as he walked
across a pasture, saw a beetle
rolling a ball of dung, and knew
he must put both bug and dung
in a poem in which he dared
to insist that not an inch
or particle of himself or anyone
else was vile and that he kept
as delicate around the bowels
as around the head and heart.

The Corn Cave

While others splashed
in the lake or sat
on the bank holding
poles with lines
at the ends of which
nightcrawlers wriggled
in the water

I slipped up the hill
and crawled into the shade
of a cave with a roof
of curved green blades
and beams of stalks.

As I sat crosslegged
between rows of corn
sunlight beat on my roof
and trickled through
onto my hands and face.

Streaked with light
I listened to cries
of cousins playing
and the low hum
of aunts and uncles
talking in chairs
beneath the walnut tree.

Corn silk grew
from ears ripening
above my head
as blades scraped
together and I
scratched the soil

between tall stalks
and picked at
the flinty fruit
of an arrowhead.

A campfire burned
where I sat in my cave
as food spiced
with herbs simmered
in clay pots

and I heard the call
in the old tongue
to come eat
at the long table

as cousins came
running and elders
stood and turned
to follow the young.

Hauling Hay

As the sun burned
on the back
of your neck

you grabbed a bale
with both hands
by the binder twine

heaved it high
enough to clear
the mounting stack
on the back
of the wagon
pulled along
by a tractor
groaning in low

someone stacked
it just right so
the whole load
somehow held
in balance

and the chaff
swirling in hot
air like a swarm
of sweat bees

settled on your
shoulder, slipped
beneath the collar
of your sweat-
sopped shirt

and pricked
the skin stretched
across your spine.

Hayloft

To grab hold of a rough rope
with both hands, push off

the edge of a stack of bales
with all your weight pulling

the line tight and swing free
feet first into the warm dark air

and land with a rich plop
on a bank of hay and roll

over on your back and look
up to see motes of dust canoeing

down a shaft of sunlight slanting
into the barn through an opening

where the elevator tip is propped
during the rush of hay-making

and to inhale the aroma
of sweet cowshit rising from

the stables below and turn over
on your side and draw your knees

up to your navel and rest
in the delicious quiet

of this warm place while
everyone is somewhere else.

Feeding the Cattle

A bale of hay balanced
on each front fender,
several more stacked
in the back of the Jeep

we ripped out toward
the pasture down the lane
from the chicken house.

Mike turned one cat's
ass in front of the first
steer and spun him
the right bale.

Hit the brakes, whipped
around in reverse, cut
another and flipped the left
bale in front of the second.

Came to a full stop
in front of a gathering
of steers whose staring
eyes took in a couple
of crazy young males.

Milk Music

Bows slurred across fiddle strings
steel guitars twanged and whined
and Hank Williams crooned
about a cheatin' heart.

Chewing her cud
the cow looked away
as if pleasure were not
to be acknowledged.

Cousin Frank
humming along
squeezed her teats
with both hands.

Warm milk splashed
with a base beat
into the bucket.

Adam Schmitt's Plums

In foul territory
on the third-base side
of the vacant lot
sloping down from
East 15th Street they
stood, those ancient
plum trees owned
by a distant relative
we had heard about
but never met.

When one of the dump
trucks with his name
scripted in white
on the green doors
would appear from nowhere
and bounce down the street
spilling dark Indiana
loam in the gutter,
we screamed "Adam Schmitt!"
scattered into the alley,
and cowered in the far
corners of the neighborhood.

Black bark cracking
away from thick trunks
against which foul balls
thudded, Adam Schmitt's
plum trees yielded horizons
of white blossoms that
spilled onto our heads
and purple fruits so lush
our fingertips ached

for the right moment
to feel and taste.

Because we never had
permission to play
on the property
of the owner we imagined
to be a bearded god-
like man of mystery

we plucked and devoured
the fruits of those
magic trees as if we
were the first to discover
the intoxicating sweetness
and terror of sin.

Forty years later
I can still feel
my teeth pop
the midnight skin
of those fleshy fruits
and taste their juices
as they anoint my lips
and tingle on this tongue
that has since found
a language for sharing
forbidden delights.

The Labor Day Boxes

At dusk we rolled
onto the sidewalks
pulling strings attached
to open shoe boxes
with crêpe paper windows,
candle-flames fluttering inside.

One year father made plywood
boxes with Tinker Toy wheels,
a hinged trapdoor, and sectioned
window frames covered with paper
patterned like stained glass.

Streaming together, we
pulled our votive flames
behind us into the dark
down the street toward
the factories where our fathers
made chairs and desks.

Like monks and nuns
in a diminutive order
we cried out a sing-
song incantation that
echoed back and forth
throughout the neighborhood,
Labor Day, Labor Day,

as rows of parents looking
down at the candlelight
rising to their faces gave
praise to our procession.

The Morning Glories

First thing
summer mornings

I would come out
to the porch,
tiptoe down the steps,
pad barefoot
across the grass

stand behind the trellis
and look up to see
how many of Mother's
morning glories
had opened.

They were so blue
and pure, beaded
with dew

as if miniature
gateways to the skies
had swayed open

allowing me
to ramble
into infinity.

The Horseradish Man

(after e. e. cummings)

Eddie and I
were playing
pitch & catch
in the vacant lot

& Susie & Sarah
were jumping rope
on the sidewalk

next to Mary Lou
& cousin Marlene
who were skipping
at hopscotch

& it was May

& old man Mehringer
was cutting his grass
with his push mower

& his Mrs. was
pinning up white wash
on the clothesline

when a man from
another neighborhood
rolled his Chevy
up to the curb

hobbled to the back
of the car
& opened his trunk.

We all stopped
what we were doing
& stared until
somebody yelled
from a front porch
"The horseradish man!"

Moms & dads
came rushing
from every direction

the Schroeders & Schuchs
from Dewey Street

the Kieffners & Kreileins
from Vine

the Kleins & the Kueblers
from East 15th.

The line formed
at the trunk
& stretched
around the corner

& it was spring

& the gates
to horseradish heaven
had sprung wide open!

When the House Was New

There were no houses
in one direction but only
weeds shagging the field
sloping down a long hill
toward a road far below
and a ditch in the middle
with saplings on either side
and rabbits jumped ahead
of your step parting prairie
grass and quails kept sending
their semaphore of a song
from a corner of the woods
and the sun burned the back
of your neck a ruddy brown
and you could roam as far
as you wanted all day long
and the bottoms of your feet
were so tough you could
walk a straight line over
an eternity of rocks
and never flinch and across
the rock road in front
of the new house was a field
of rye which evening breezes
riffled and transformed
from light green to darker
blue and when the sun
started to sink on the other
side of the house a fire
lit up the sky and as you
toppled into bed you knew
you would roll over
and the morning would come
to meet you again as soon
as you opened your eyes.

Woods Hymn

Where the path crossed
on a log the creek
flowed after a rain.
Treetops shifted
and dripped
in the breeze.

I stood deep
in those woods,
eyes wide open
for the shapes
of leaves, ears
tuned to the cries
of birds and cuttings
of fox squirrels.

To look was
to affirm a faith
I felt particular
to the place.

To see was
to receive
a grace I could
not define.

To hear was
to know a music
that could not
be written down.

To breathe the air
of the woods was
to give thanks for

what was there
and nowhere else

and stood in need
of no thanks for
being what it was.

Bloodroot

I have seen
a light green
leaf, closely
coiled around
a stalk, emerge
through winter
brown leaves.

A flower rose
above, white
as fresh snow
atop a mountain.

Eight oval petals
opened like
parts of an eye
eager to behold
all that's new.

I dug and scratched
the rootstock
and saw a red
juice out of which
Potawatomi boiled
tea to bathe burns
and settlers squeezed
onto a lump of sugar
they held in the mouth
to cure sore throat.

White petals,
open again beneath
my eyelids.

Leathery leaves,
rub against
my fingertips.

Red potion,
cure this tongue
and move it
toward praise
of your powers.

The Blackberry Bramble

When you hear the dull
concussion of Fourth
of July firecrackers
down the hill you
know the time is right.

With a gallon bucket
in either hand walk
beyond the house
down the logging path
beyond the bend
to the side of which
your first rabbit trap
will stand raised
on a wooden platform
when the season opens.

Carry on to the edge
of the far side
of the woods, but not
so far as to the felled
trees beside which
pokeberries cluster
and quail roosting
in a circle explode
into flight as you approach.

Leave the path
there on the right:
enter the bramble.

Chiggers advance
to the coal oil
ringing your ankles.

The long-sleeved
work shirt you wear
hunting fox squirrels
deeper in summer
insulates you from
mosquitoes buzzing
your ears and the bill
of your baseball cap.

Reach out first
with your eyes.
Give thanks before
allowing yourself
to touch.

Let the midnight
black ripeness
surrender to
your fingertips,
cover the bottom
of one bucket
with mounds of
building sweetness,
pile toward the top
of the container
growing in gravity.

* * *

Walled in within
this thicket
of early abundance

inhale the aroma
of pie baking
in the oven

and cobbler cooling
on the sill
of an open window
in the kitchen.

As first snow settles
on branches beyond
the frosting panes,
run your tongue
along black jelly
smeared across
buttered toast.

* * *

Savor this humming
quietness you have
found and cultivated.
Stay still.

The bramble which
encloses you
will soon crumble
to ashes.

A bulldozer will
grade and taper
the hill. A house
will rise. Grass
will germinate
and poke through
a layer of straw.

Sassafras

Along railroad tracks
you flex a waxy
awkward mitten
on one hand
and with another
offer egg-smooth
ovals of green
to the sun.

Rub your leaves
or bark between
fingers and inhale
the fragrance
concealed behind
the ear of
an empress.

Dry your leaves,
mash into powder,
sprinkle as filé
in a bowl of gumbo
and stay young
like the Cajuns.

I have sipped
the juice of
the bark of
your roots
boiled in water
on a drizzly
winter day and
felt summer sun
burn in my veins.

Queen Anne's Lace

Against a galaxy
of dark greens

this constellation
of whites

within which
tiny stars

pulse the color
of an old

rusty fence
beside which

we stand
and gaze.

White Oak

Leaves lobed
like the inlets
of the lakes
around which
raccoons forage
in moonlight

pulp of your
bowl-shaped fruit
sweet enough to
satisfy the tooth
of the Piankashaw
and fatten wild boars

squirrels scampered
home to the dens
in your trunk
in the thinning
forests I hunted
with my father

and my grandfather
still shakes his head
as he guides the teeth
of his whirling saw

into your prime
flesh on the farms
of his neighbors.

His Only Hickory Sapling

He was short,
he was quiet,
he was gentle,

but when he found
the only hickory sapling
on the hilltop property
he had just bought

chopped down by loggers
working in the woods
beyond our lot to clear
a lane to the rock road
in front of the site
where he would put
up a new house
for his family

my father rose
to a mighty
large-leafed anger.

He nailed a note
to a stake he pounded
into the ground
between white chips
they had scattered

calling them a rough
name I had never
heard come out
of his mouth.

As I later stood
on those white chips
shaping the sounds
of the words he had
slashed in black ink
on white paper

my father grew
taller than the largest
shagbark hickory
in the forest where
we hunted squirrels

and I felt how
deep his roots
turned and twisted
into the ground.

The Martin Box

Every spring when he
announced the time
was right we raised

and fastened the pole
atop of which stood
the tiered house

of many apartments
he had built of wood
and painted white

with green trim. We
waited for the first
purple martin to drop

onto the wrapped-
around porch and collect
bits of straw and cloth

for a nest in one
of the compartments.
Before long we would

hear the squeak
of the young
and the mother

would dive as
I cut the grass
with a power mower

and raise goosebumps
up and down the back
of my tanned neck.

But then they stopped
coming back and
the compartments

stayed empty and
quiet and my father
stood on the lawn

staring at the sky
in which hung
clouds of silence

and he walked away
with eyes dropped
to the ground.

The Potato Barrows

Where trees had
once stood and she
pulled out the stumps

he pushed the plow
along the mound
he had heaped.

I followed with
a bucket of cut
spuds I placed

eyes up at
intervals before
she came along

and folded the dark
earth at the edge
of the woods

back over them.
I watched green
stalks and leaves

push out into
sunlight and white
flowers open.

When the stalks
lost their green
and withered

she sent me with
a shovel and pail
to dig up enough

for a meal.
With the tip
of the tool

I pried loose
the underground fruit,
touched their tender

skin and later
broke into white
flesh with a fork

after she boiled
them on the stove.
Later after we

rolled them out
of their long
barrows with

the prongs of
the plow we
hauled them

in bushel baskets
in procession
into the basement.

We laid them
out on newspaper
for the winter

and came back
to find the survivors
sprouting eyes

in the dark,
as daylight expanded,
ready to be

quartered
and set back
in the ancestral

mounds to bloom
again at the edge
of the woods.

Gathering Hickory Nuts

After the first hard frost
we packed into the Chevy.
Father drove slowly along
a winding road, into the hills.
We squirmed in the back seat
as rocks kicked up against
the bottom of the car.

When we finally arrived
at the Blessinger farm
we coasted into a field
across the road from
the sloping woods and parked
beneath a black walnut tree.

Burlap bags slung across
our shoulders like wings,
we flushed from the car
like a covey of quail,
glided down the hill
between tall trees, and came
to alight beneath the first
shagbark hickory that had
splattered its hard fruit
on the frosted forest floor.

We stuffed our bags
with the hard white nuts
that emerge like pearls
when the brittle green husks
hit ground and split apart.

The deeper we drifted down
the hills, the heavier our harvest.

At the bottom of the hill where
woods opened into pasture
we turned, balanced our loads
on our shoulders and headed
back toward the car.

The darkness following us from
the pasture pressed against our
backs and pushed us up the hill
as we rushed to reach the far
field where light still flickered
and faded on the empty Chevy.

At the edge of the woods
Mother picked orange-eyed
bittersweet to stick in a jug
in a corner of the living room.

We surrendered our treasure
of nuts to the trunk and drifted
back down the hills in the dark
to the warmth of home
like an old ship provisioned
for a long hard voyage.

The Quilters

They took turns coming to one
another's houses in the winter,

my relatives and neighbors,
and I remember the long frame

from the farmhouse we stored
in the attic and would set up

in the living room we usually
kept closed off and unheated.

We pulled the curtains back
and opened the vents and they

sat facing one another, three
to a side, stitching and talking,

pausing only to roll the fabric
tight around one pole when

the stitching overtook the unquilted
space between them. Thy broke

for dinner at noon, moved to
the kitchen table where they

chewed, smiled and talked before
returning to the living room to stitch

and tell stories through the afternoon,
broke off at five for soup in the kitchen

where they sipped and klatsched,
then stitched and gossiped well

into the dark and it seemed every line
and space had been thoroughly stitched

and every story completely told and they
laughed and said good-bye and good night

and the house shrunk back into silence
after the last quilter had gone out

the back door. Later in my bed I saw
again the movements of the needles

and heard the tongues still stitching
their common quilt of memory.

The Rock-Hitter

He scrapes his feet back and forth
into position beside the plate outlined
in the rock road. In left, the lawn,
the house, and an orchard for stands.
Center is the telephone line looped
across the road where the neighbor's
property begins. Right is a blue-
green field of rye with the woods
as screened-off pavilion. A bob-
white calls from the briars beyond.

With right hand he grips the stake
at the tapered end, with left flips
a rock into the middle of the strike zone,
joins hands together, and pulls a screamer
across the lawn that scorches leaves
off the pear trees. He flips another,
swings later, and sends it rising
on a line toward center where a turtle
dove flaps up from the telephone
line and wings into the woods.

He turns around, now Musial
the lefty, crouches into a corkscrew
stance, swings earlier, and hooks
a flat one that hums across the tips
of rye stalks. As it strikes
a briar patch beyond, a covey
of quail explodes into flight.

See those quail rise, soar
and glide into the woods.
Watch the boy jog around the bases,
tip his cap, and bow after

he jumps onto home plate.

Watch him turn around again,
age, and pick up a pen.
Feel his grip tighten around
the bottom of that stick.

Listen to him stroke lines
that reach all the way back
to rye, orchard, and woods.

Saturday Night at the Calumet

When the band from Louisville
cranked up the rockabilly,
the girls sprang from their chairs
and danced onto the floor.

The guys stood back along
their tables and poured drinks
from bottles they had stashed
in their sportcoat pockets.

The later it got, the stronger
the drinks, the longer the songs.
When the band lapsed into a slow one,
boys ventured onto the floor with girls.

Lights grew dimmer, smoke thicker,
and the hardwood floor pulsed
on piles above muddy lake water
as tempers flared toward the last dance.

When the band pulled their plugs,
lights flashed back on, and the lead
singer and his backups left
the hall with their first choices.

Someone always wanted to fight,
someone always got sick in the lot,
and two daredevils always played
chicken on the road back into town.

Because I Could Not Stop

(after Emily Dickinson)

It was well past midnight
after the Saturday night dance.
I had no idea where I was going,
or why, but could not stop
myself from taking a ride.

My father's car held only me.
No friend came along to drive,
but Someone sat at my side.

That car sped due south,
no destination in sight or mind,
along the only straight stretch
between the slumping hills.

I leaned toward the wheel
squinting ahead. All I could see,
in my boozy blur, was a needle
standing with its back pressed
up against a glowing 120.

Seems like aeons ago the hood
of that car was aimed at infinity.

How or why I survived that
desperate drive long enough to
tell this foolish tale I have no clue.

I only know that somewhere—
between there and here—
I grabbed the pen, shifted
from gear to gear, and drove
deeper and deeper into the dark

before turning around to
head back toward the light.

Song for Bob Dylan
(1971)

The restless little
Midwestern creature
with reflecting eyes
tingling antennae
& scraping cry
secretes himself in
a new myth for each
winter & then drops
out & wings away
to another tree just
as his followers
begin to wriggle
in the cocoon
that's fallen behind.

III

Odysseus in Indiana

Odysseus in Indiana

Back in the hills again after
twenty years of wanderlust
on an island far to the east:
the home place is in bad shape.

The best squirrel-hunting woods
in the county stripped of giant
shagbark hickories and white oaks
by logging crews from somewhere else.

An asphalt parking lot stretching
toward infinity from shops in a mall
blackens the fields where my favorite
setters pointed coveys of quail.

Prefab houses arranged in rows
where my best rabbit traps tripped,
the river in which I caught sweet
catfish percolates like leftover

coffee heated by the chemicals
factories dump down its banks.
Basketball goals shorn of nets
tilt off center, ragged weeds grow

where I fielded hot grounders
and cracked hard line drives.
Lamentation and loss lie
like a blight across the land.

The fingerprints of old friends
run up and down both barrels
of my twelve gauge and the key
to the walnut gun case is gone.

In the corner of the bedroom
on the smooth oak floor I laid
sprawls a delicate nightgown
whose threads are unravelled.

In the taverns where they barely
recognize me because of the gray
streaking my beard and the tinge
of Eastern intonation in my voice

they tell me my old sweetheart
the cheerleader got tired of waiting
and left town with the all-state hotshot
from the burg across the valley.

Nettles grow all over my father's grave.
My mother sometimes forgets my name.
The old place was bulldozed and burned.
Nobody around to speak the old language.

I was a damned fool to come back.
You can go back home, all right,
but what you find there is always less
than what you thought you left behind.

Old Man in a Small-Town Tavern

Drifted into a small town
founded by a missionary,
named after a bishop,
where my brother owned
a tavern and served the best
fried chicken and German
fries in the county.

My brother was out,
the bartender said,
so I pulled up a stool,
ordered a tall schooner,
sat watching the suds
slide down the sides
of the pearl-frost mug.

Smell of onions
sizzling in the kitchen.

Heard a lot of old songs
in the back of my mind,
thought of a lot of people,
wondered where they
all might have gone.

Side door swung open
and in hobbled an old
man bent over a cane
but wearing a smile.
Had shaved the shadow
off his wrinkled face
just for the occasion.

Knew him at once!

Silas, father of no son
or daughter, yet somehow
a second father to me,
man who taught me how
to hunt in his own woods,

had heard I was back,
had drifted down
from the farm at the top
of the highest hill
to the tavern where
he thought I might stop.

His large hand felt
both tough and soft
to the shake.

His eyes still
had the old glow,
his slow speech
the old accent.

We both sensed
our time together
was at a premium.

A song about country roads
pulsed on the Wurlitzer.

I could still hear
that gray squirrel bark
on a branch of a black
walnut in the back
of his woods as I tried
to sneak in for a shot.

I still pointed a long
flashlight at his side
into the oak tree
beneath which his 'coon
hound barked treed.

I watched the frost
on my mug turn clear
as the occasional bubble
rose toward the top.

I tried to savor the taste
of what was left,
but the last few sips
had a hard, bitter bite.

Return to a Mighty Fortress

in memory of Jack London Leas

College kids home
for the vacation
in the small town
in the hills, we gather
in the house of our
mentor, Jack the Ripper.

Beer, Beethoven, more beer,
and then Bach: Toccata and Fugue
in D Minor rattles the front windows.

But to listen to E. Power
Biggs boom it out on a record
playing on a stereo in a living
room is not the same as hearing
the master played by someone
you know in a church built
of sandstone hauled from a farm
beside the banks of the Patoka River
by German-Catholic pioneers
whose names you inherited.

So we pile in Ripper's car
and lurch toward the Romanesque
fortress with the Tower of London
in the center of town, St. Joseph's
Church, where we were all
baptized and confirmed.

My musical friend who
several years later choked
off his life with a belt around

his neck has the key from
the old choirmaster, Professor
Loepker, and opens the doors
and the mighty console.

We sit in sudsy piety
where at Midnight Mass
every Christmas Eve
since early childhood we
have listened to the ethereal
tenor of Maury Gutgsell
sing "Stille Nacht"
and "Adeste Fidelis."

Jeff warms up with
"Tantum Ergo," plays
"Jesus, Joy of My Heart's
Desire." We applaud,
but know it's not enough.

Ripper, a late convert
to German Catholicism,
claims he hasn't touched
an organ in years, but we
know when the time is right
and prod him up the stairs
to the choir loft and beg
for that Protestant anthem
we Catholics covet,
"A Mighty Fortress Is Our God."

"Sacrilege!" Ripper chortles
as he hits the first key and brings
Martin Luther alive in the House
of Indiana German-Catholicism.

The pipes expand as he
builds to a mighty crescendo
and Catholic dust settles
on our heads and shoulders
as we rise to our feet
and applaud wildly
the musical wizardry
of the man who just
a few years before had
peered down at us from
his desk over reading glasses
to inform us exactly where
we should have put
the required comma
in the compound sentence.

Song for a Sister

Back at the site of your tiny tomb,
sister, still not sure what to say.

First fact: Born Jan. 25, 1950.
Second fact: Died Jan. 25, 1950.
This year you would have turned 45.

They named you Marilyn,
but you may have been gone
by the time the name was given.
Or perhaps the name was selected
and waiting like a baptismal
gown sewn for you to fit into.

I don't know whether to say
you died in being born
or were already dead
before you could be born.

Let's just say your death
coincided with your birth
and that I never saw you.

I believe in you nonetheless.
Perhaps I miss you more
for never having met you.

Whenever I return from
the Island in the East
I come back to your small
stone on which it is carved:
GONE TO BE AN ANGEL.

Halcyon times, the time
of your birth and death,
the pundits tell us,
but I remember our mother's
grief all too well, the sound
of her sobs descending the stairs
from the bedroom in which
her mother scolded her hard.

Grandma's husband, you may know,
left her and this world at age 33
with six young children on the farm.
No time for self-pity. Pigs to feed
and butcher. Meals to cook,
clothes to wash, crops to put in.

Our father swallowed his grief
over the loss of a daughter,
carried it for years.
It had to tear at his guts.

Marilyn, I have concluded
that in talking to you
I speak to that part of myself
I have not been lucky enough
to discover but which will one
day rejoin and complete me.

The green grass of summer
grows around your clean-carved,
well-trimmed tombstone
not far from the tall tomb
of the maternal ancestor
who came from Lohr am Main.

To return here
from far away

and try to preserve
even the slightest trace
of you is to pay
tribute to a life so dear
its mysterious end
arrived as it began.

The Dropped Pigskin

for Mick and Mary Ellen Stenftenagel

Broke through a big hole
in the line into the open
with nothing but long white
stripes and my first touchdown
coming toward me.

Looked back
and found my best friend Mick
had laid a perfect spiral into the air
spinning toward me in slow motion.

Watched it smack my hands
and fall to the ground.

Had to turn and run back
to the huddle past the subs
and our young coach
from Western Kentucky
who spoke with a drawl
thicker than autumn mist
hovering in the hollows.

"Son!" he yelled in my ear,
his voice rising above the din
of the crowd like the bay
of a hound that's finally
treed an ornery 'coon
after chasing it across
the whole damn woods,
"you ever do that agin
I'm mo slit yore throat!"

He didn't have to.

Second half Mick
cranked it up again.

I broke open, he spun
the pigskin into the air,
I hauled it in and heaved
it underhanded into the air
as I jumped into the end zone
and came back to solid earth.

Coach stood on the sidelines,
cocked his Kentucky head
to the side, nodded, pounded
absolution with his palms.

Letter from Mattingly Country

Along the banks
of the Ohio River
at the end of a summer
when the water sank
as low as the spirit
of a man who's lost
his job and doesn't know
how he can feed the family
you could feel the surge
of pride and relief
as the bat came alive
and the team came closer:

the man who carries
himself in our quiet way,
speaks the language
with our Hoosier accent,
plays this country's greatest
game in the intense old style,
gives it all he's got
and always a little more,
has made it into October.

So maybe the bat doesn't
crack as loud as it did
before the back blew out.
So maybe the numbers
are down from the time
he was the kid from Evansville
who turned every baseball
head from the Bronx to L.A.
by turning every other pitch
into a vicious line drive

that rocketed into or over
outfield walls in every city.

He can still flash the gold-
glove leather like nobody else.
He can still pick the right
moment to torque his sore back
and rip the ball off the foul pole

and when he comes back
to the dugout there isn't a single
rookie or veteran or coach,
including the manager, who
doesn't want to touch his hand.

Here along the banks
of the rising Ohio River
we don't need New York
sportswriters to explain to us
why hard-nosed fans in the Bronx
still stand when he steps
into the batter's box even
though the numbers are down.

Here along the banks
of the Ohio River
we always knew that spirit
and class count double,
that Don Mattingly
would one day make it
to eternal October.

Dream of a Hanging Curve

When I see it spinning
like a Florida grapefruit
toward me, let me not
lunge at it like a rookie.

If it's outside, help me
shift my weight and lash
it to the opposite field.

If it should come down
the middle, let me send it
right back where it came
from, but harder and faster.

If it comes toward the inside corner,
give me the patience to wait,
turn on it, and pull it down
the line to kick up chalk
and carom around in the corner.

If I should have the luck
to make the right connection,
follow through perfectly
and see the ball rise
in an arc that will end
somewhere behind the fence,
let me not take too long
to circle the bases, gesture
toward the other dugout,
jump onto home plate,
or high-five everyone in sight
while the pitcher hangs his head.

If this dream comes true,
do not let me expect it
will ever happen again.

Do not let me change what
I have been doing that
got me to where I am.

Let me stay here as long
as I can give what I have
been given to contribute.

Let me be remembered
for what I became,
not for what I might
or should have been.

Return to a Grape Arbor

Back home visiting my mother
in the swelter of Indiana August
I walk into the garden where
rows of Dad's potatoes grew until
we grew up and moved away.

Around the edge of the plot,
now only one quarter tilled
for the few vegetables she can
tend and eat, his Concord grapes
twine around the wires he stretched
between poles sunk into cement.

Many bruise-blue clusters
shriveled and dropped
to the ground. Bees buzz
between leaves browning
at the edge. Too many
bunches still hang unspoiled.
Seventeen years since his fingers
plucked the fruit of these vines.

Nobody to trim or pick these
grapes, nobody to make the wine
or jelly. Only the smaller thirst
and appetite of one where there
was once a much fuller six.

So I return to the kitchen
for a knife and dishpan,
take off my New York watch,
step back deep into the arbor
to reach, cut, and preserve
what can only fall to waste.

It feels good to cut at the right
point on the stem and let his fruit
fall to the bottom of the pan.

Memories of sweet reddish-blue
wine we siphoned from oak barrels
tingle on my tongue. I see him
lift his glass, sip, say how
good it tastes, and sigh.

Just as I savor the tangy
flavor of memory, the knife slips,
gashes my thumb, and blood
mingles with the sweetness
glazing my fingertips.

Dorothy and the Jewish Coat

Before Clara entered the convent
in Indiana she cleaned and cooked
for the Rosenfeld family in Louisville.

When Clara's brother-in-law Frank,
my grandfather, died young and left
Mary, my grandmother, with six young

children, Clara told the Rosenfelds
and they sent a care package of used
clothes to the farm in southern Indiana.

Dorothy, six, got a good coat
which kept her warm and almost
happy during that first hard winter.

One Sunday after mass Dorothy
stopped in town to visit her mother's
parents; and the uncles teased her

about her new old coat. "Oh I
would never wear that coat,"
one taunted. "Jews stink!"

Seventy-five years later my mother
tells me the story of how she cooked
and cleaned for two Jewish families

in Louisville after graduating from
high school and remembers, as if it
happened yesterday, how sharply

she felt the sting of an uncle's hate
whenever she wore the Jewish coat
that kept her warm in the winter.

The Mandolin and the Tenor

for Frank Schmitt

Winter nights when animal breath
hung frozen in the barn
you gathered wife and six
children around the wood stove
in the old farmhouse,

picked a delicate, haunting
tune on that most American
of instruments, the mandolin,

and lifted your tenor toward
the cold Indiana heavens
as you sang for the family
that most German love song
of loss, *Du, du liegst
mir im Herzen.*

I never heard your tenor,
Grandfather Frank, never saw
the mandolin kept in a closet
until it became a toy children
wore out, but the long-gone
instrument still resonates

as your daughter, eighty-three,
tells me again the story of your life
and sings for me your sad German
song in her most frail of voices.

In return, I sing this song
of her loss of a father when
you were thirty-three. She

was only six. Your oldest child,
my godfather, was only twelve.

I leave you singing *Stille Nacht,*
heilige Nacht in your heavenly
tenor in the choir loft of the village
church on Christmas Eve and repeat
as your epitaph this refrain:
Du, du liegst mir im Herzen.*

                              * You're still in my heart.

Let Morning Light

After the hard winter night,
when north wind whipped
against this house, let morning
light come out of the east
and find its way to the kitchen
table where she sits, in clean
clothes, lifting oatmeal, slowly,
to her mouth with a spoon.

Let sips of coffee wake her
to the core and send heat
all the way to her nose
and tips of arthritic fingers.

Let her walk, step by step,
into the sunroom, pull open
the curtains, sit down
in a recliner, and watch the sun
rise higher and brighter as she
listens to local news on the radio.

Let her fall asleep in the chair,
if medication pulls her down,
and wake up when an old friend
calls to see how she feels,
or when it is time to sit down
at the table for the main meal.

After the dishes are washed, let her
settle down in the white oak rocker
beside the southern window,
facing the woods, and bask
in the sunlight warming her face.
Let the branches of winter trees
cross in a pattern that pulls her

back to her childhood on the farm.

As the sun passes along behind
the house, turns the corner,
and reappears in the west,
let afternoon light intensify
through the window in her bedroom
and warm the covers on the bed
into which she may crawl for a nap.
Let the quilt whose patches
she cut out and sewed together
rise and fall as she breathes.

Let the dusk bound softly
toward the house, the dark
fall gently, and the night surround
the house but relent. Let the light
come out of the east again and find
her sitting in clean clothes at the table.

Hugging the Spirit

Odysseus followed Circe's advice,
sailed north into cold shadows,
offered warm blood to raise the spirits.

Thus he found his mother, who had died
while he wandered. He longed to hug her,
to hold her close, but could not reach her,

whom he loved so much, whose voice
spoke his name across the abyss. For even
when spirit is as close as the heartbeat

in your chest, you cannot reach out
and touch it. You must honor the distance,
even as you feel the pulse of the cord.

So I flew back home, Mother, and found you
in your reclining chair in the corner of the room
where morning light enters. You rose, shakily,

out of the shadows. I put my arms around
what I could find of you, held what was left
of your flesh, and kissed your thinning lips.

It was like kissing the mist in the valleys.
I saw faint light flicker in your sunken eyes.
I knew I could not hold you for long.

I had to let you return to the shadows.
I sat and watched you labor to breathe
with your eyes closed. I played a tape

I made of songs you loved, in the old tongue.
I saw your lips shape some of the words.
Once you voiced a line in a high register,

and almost smiled. I knew you were sailing
back to rejoin the father who died when
you were but a little girl. It was as clear

as the sunlight that you were ready to go.
I tried not to hold on too long, for I knew
that spirit cannot be contained in one world.

Farewell Lullaby

Lay your weary head,
poor sick mother,
on my shoulder.

Soon you shall rest.
Soon you shall hear
the mandolin music
you loved as a girl.

No, nothing you ever
said or did could cause
sickness and suffering
like what you endure.

Soon, soon you shall rest.
Soon these trials shall pass.

Soon the wrinkles
on your forehead and face
shall disappear like snow
when warm sun shines.

Soon the smile shall return
to your thinning lips like
the wildflowers that appear
each spring in the woods
where you played as a girl.

Soon you shall hear,
once again so clear,
the fatherly tenor
that slipped into silence
when you were so young.

Lay your weary head,
poor sick mother,
on this shoulder
as light from afar comes
to rest on your face.

At Least Now

At least now
she does not have to
try to catch her breath
swallow food hard
suck ice to wet
her parched throat
struggle to get out
one more word
on the phone.

At least now
she does not have to
worry about whether
the stove is still on
the bills are paid
or if there is enough
cash in her purse
or the back of the drawer
to buy more groceries.

At least now
she does not have to
be embarrassed about
the memory that crashed
and the hair that fell out
or care about the wrinkles
that wrapped around her face
or the flesh that vanished
from her bones.

At least now
she does not have to
fear the cold that found her
no matter how high

the furnace was set
or how close
the electric heater roared.

At least now
that she has graduated
to pure spirit she can
soar where she wants,
perch on our shoulders
and come along
wherever we go.

The Reunion

My father sits
hunched over
on a stone bench
as my mother's
shadow approaches.

He looks up
in surprise, says:
"Oh, I didn't know
you were coming!"

"It took me so long!"
She sighs. He moves
over to make room,
Mother settles down
beside him once more,

and they give
one another
the kind of airy
embrace spirits
offer when they
find themselves
together again
in the same world.

"Isn't that bird
song beautiful?" she
asks. "Yes," he
answers, "but it's
so different from
what we knew."

She tries to whistle
a reply to the song
she hears, but
the melody that floats
out of her mouth
is pure abstraction.

Odysseus in the Rain

1

Driving south in the rain
one more time to pick up
the balance of what I
claim as my legacy

from the old family place,
now another family's home,
I see, between cycles
of windshield wiper swishes,

streaks of redbud in bloom
alternating with dogwood white
above patches of mayapple green
on either side of limestone bluffs.

The home town is at the far end
of a channel through the hills
where I am pulled in this season
of birth and time of death.

2

At the grave site on the hill
we find her name and dates
carved next to my father's.
In the attached vases

we find silk daffodils.
Mother, soon we return
with fresh blue irises, streaked
with yellow, and yellow daisies,

and you come alive again for us,
you who loved to tend flowers,
loved the feel of dirt,
hummed as you worked.

3

My son and I walk the banks
of a muddy, swollen Patoka.
For the first time, we stay
in a motel in my home town.

In the middle of the night,
the phone rings: tornado watch,
everyone out in the hall.
Our teenage daughter, fighting

mononucleosis, though we don't
yet know it, sobs that she "wants
to go home." Her mother hugs her;
I walk to a door with a fellow traveler

and watch lightning crackle across
southern skies. Gray clouds stacked
everywhere. Why do I always love
storms? Who knows where home is?

4

Sun shines again in morning calm.
With my grandfather's white oak rocker,
the small oak table you bought for two dollars
in the thirties when you started your first job,

and the copper "coal-packer" in which you
canned vegetables and fruits wedged
in the back of the Swedish station wagon,
we head north again, before we turn east,

to journey back to our Island home east
of New York City. The local radio
station warns us of flash floods
in low-lying areas, especially near Shoals.

We watch the East Fork of the White River
swelling where yesterday were valleys.
Lanes leading to farmhouses we cannot see
disappear into the swirling waters.

Redbuds and dogwoods still droop.
Just before we climb a hill to wind
toward Bedford, the waters swell to
the edge of the road like memories

that will wash over the road,
recede in the sun, and return
to channels cut deep into the earth
where the darkest waters collect.

Epilogue: Places

Some of my ancestors were
hired hands in fields along a river;

others worked on boats
carrying cargo downstream.

I was born and grew up
inland in the hills.

I have lived as an adult
on a fish-shaped island

and I shall return
deep into woods

in which spirits rise
like spring water

and meander downhill
over sandstone.

The Author

© 2000, 2002 by Andreas Riedel

Norbert Krapf grew up in Jasper, Indiana, a German community, moved to Long Island in 1970, and has since taught at Long Island University, where he directs the C.W. Post Poetry Center. A graduate of St. Joseph's College (Rensselaer, IN), which awarded him an honorary doctorate, he received his M.A. and Ph.D. in English and American Literature from the University of Notre Dame. His poetry volumes include the trilogy *Somewhere in Southern Indiana, Blue-Eyed Grass: Poems of Germany,* and *Bittersweet Along the Expressway: Poems of Long Island.* He is the editor of *Finding the Grain,* a collection of pioneer German journals and letters from his native Dubois County, and *Under Open Sky,* a gathering of writings by contemporary American poets on William Cullen Bryant. He is also the translator/editor of *Shadows on the Sundial: Selected Early Poems of Rainer Maria Rilke* and *Beneath the Cherry Sapling: Legends from Franconia.* A winner of the Lucille Medwick Memorial Award from The Poetry Society of America for "Fire and Ice," a poem in this volume, he has been a U.S. Exchange Teacher at West Oxon Technical College, England, and Fulbright Professor of American Poetry at the Universities of Freiburg and Erlangen-Nuremberg, Germany. For more information, see www.krapfpoetry.com.

The Photographer

Darryl Jones was born and grew up in northern Indiana, lived for sixteen years in Indianapolis, and now lives in southern Indiana. He is best known for his photography for the books *Indiana, Indiana II,* and *Indianapolis,* his postcards depicting Indiana, and his collaboration with novelist James Alexander Thom, *The Spirit of the Place: Indiana Hill Country.* Jones' photography is also included in *The Simple and Vital Design: Indiana Post Office Murals* and the recent *Destination Indiana: Travels through Hoosier History.* His photography has been exhibited in Indianapolis, Chicago, Cleveland, Boston and New York.

Jones, who cites the nature writings of Thoreau and Emerson and Chinese landscapes as influences, has said, "In a sense, what I've been trying to do is convey to Hoosiers, and then to other people who are coming to the state, what it has to offer. I think there's an inherent beauty in the landscape." In the "Photographer's Preface" to *The Spirit of the Place,* which includes "Cornfield at Sunset,"* reproduced on the cover of this book, he says, "The beauty of Indiana is often found in its subtlety, which forces the viewer to be more responsive to what is before him."

* "Cornfield at Sunset, C.R. 600 S. Near Freeman, Owen County" was previously published in *The Spirit of the Place: Indiana Hill Country,* Indiana University Press, 1995.

About the Type

This collection was typeset in Caslon, originally released by William Caslon in 1722. Because of their incredible practicality, his designs met with instant success. Caslon's types became popular throughout Europe and the American colonies; printer Benjamin Franklin used hardly any other typeface. The first printings of the American Declaration of Independence and the Constitution were set in Caslon.

Book design and typesetting by JTC Imagineering.

MAR 2 1 2003